The Present Hour

AND

In a Piece of Broken Mirror

YVES BONNEFOY

Translated and Introduced by

BEVERLEY BIE BRAHIC

Seagull
BOOKS

LONDON NEW YORK CALCUTTA

I am grateful to the editors of the following magazines where some of these translations first appeared: *Modern Poetry in Translation* ('Low Branches', 'Be Love and Psyche'); *PN Review* ('The Present Hour'); *The White Review* ('The Missing Name', 'The Revolution the Night', 'He Goes Off').

Beverley Bie Brahic

INDIA

This work is published with the support of
Institut français en Inde – Embassy of France in India

Seagull Books, 2020

L'heure présente by Yves Bonnefoy © Mercure de France, 2011
Raturer outre by Yves Bonnefoy © Éditions Galilée, 2010
'Dans un débris de miroir' in *Dans un débris de miroir* by Yves Bonnefoy
© Éditions Galilée, 2006

First published in English translation by Seagull Books, 2013
English Translation © Beverley Bie Brahic, 2013

ISBN 978 0 8574 2 753 3

British Library Cataloguing-in-Publication Data
A catalogue record for this book is available from the British Library

Typeset by Seagull Books, Calcutta, India
Printed and bound by WordsWorth India, New Delhi, India

CONTENTS

INTRODUCTION

What a rare pleasure it is for a translator to offer a complete collection of poems—not a tasting menu—especially one in which each poem is in conversation with all the other poems. Of course, all the discrete parts of Yves Bonnefoy's considerable *oeuvre* (poems, essays on art and aesthetics, translations) are in conversation with one another but it is especially moving to see this at the level of a single collection of poems, here *The Present Hour*.

The Present Hour contains sonnet sequences, an extended meditation in free verse from which the collection takes its title and a number of prose poems—or 'récits en rêve' (dream tales)[1]—the last of which, the volume's three-part closing text, pushes through metaphoric brushwood towards death (finitude and transcendence, not religious or super-natural, are recurring questions in Bonnefoy's works) and weighs a life spent grappling with words 'that shrivel under our pens . . . big splintery words, that scrape us . . . words whose tangles dissimulate holes, into which we slip and slide . . .'

Throughout this volume, autobiographical elements point towards subliminal narratives: an apparently impersonal poem about a work of art, a painting by Max Ernst, for instance, may suddenly lurch towards the personal, collaging events and emotions that seem to originate not in the painting but in the 'forbidden cupboards' (as Bonnefoy writes in *The Arrière-pays* [2]) of his own childhood: the sonnets, especially, can bring to

[1] This is the subtitle of Yves Bonnefoy's collection of prose poems, *Rue Traversière* (Beverley Bie Brahic trans.) (London: Seagull Books, 2016).

mind those jigsaw puzzles based on reproductions of paintings, into which pieces from another landscape, more personal, have been surreptitiously mixed, the first person entering unexpectedly and exiting just as suddenly.

In his many discussions of poetic technique, Bonnefoy emphasizes the importance of the sense of sound and of composing with both the ear and the unconscious; he praises the secret life of words. The poems in *The Present Hour* call to one another in their vocables, their touchstone words—*safre*, *chevêche*, to mention two, with the aura of proper nouns—as well as in motif and theme. And if poetic form in *The Present Hour* varies from prose texts to discursive free verse to the condensed, elliptical, frequently enigmatic sonnets (unrhymed; Bonnefoy, a close reader of Baudelaire, Rimbaud and Mallarmé, does not think that the constraints of rhyme have a place here and, perhaps, not at all in contemporary poetry), the poems' tone is consistently lyrical or philosophical–lyrical; the language by and large is what we, English readers, would consider 'elevated', whence, perhaps, the awe in which Bonnefoy is held. In the preface to a recent translation, Bonnefoy speaks of the 'irreducible' features of languages with particular reference to French and English, and admires the latter's aptitude 'for the observation of concrete detail at a specific place and time, otherwise put, for the expression of the events of a particular existence . . . In French poetry, we just don't have that easy continuity between the ultimate ends and the most immediate social reality . . .'[3]

2 Bonnefoy, *The Arrière-pays* (Stephen Romer trans.) (London: Seagull Books, 2012), pp. 98–100.

3 Bonnefoy, *Beginning and End of the Snow* (Emily Grosholz trans.) (Lanham, MD, Plymouth, UK: Bucknell University Press, 2012), pp. x–xii.

*

Translating Yves Bonnefoy into English is challenging on several accounts. Bonnefoy uses a pared-down, elemental diction, but which may have philosophical reach, especially in hard-to-translate terms such as *évidence* and *présence*. In some remarks made in 2006 about Paul Valéry, Bonnefoy tells of seeking

> to experience the connection between the ordinary word—the big ordinary word designative of the big simple realities, the wind, the tree, the cold, the stone— and its inevitable becoming-concept, but also its vocation for resurrection, for presence.[4] 'To experience in the words their immobility, their congealing into concept, but also their return to movement, to life. Gain access to poetry's gaze not by way of figures building for us, hastily, beautiful images, but in each vocable's thickness, a thickness whose foundation, under the drift of the signifieds, is what one calls the referent.'[5]

The word-concept-theme-metaphor *lumière* (light) recurs, for example, and the translator is tempted to find 'grittier' substitutes—glow, sheen, glimmer, glitter, etc.—according to the context, words less abstract, more in the style of English poetry's

---

[4] 'Presence' for Bonnefoy seems to have almost Buddhist overtones of learning to exist in the here and now, rather than yearning towards an unattainably ideal 'over there'. Stephen Romer, in the introduction to his translation of *The Arrière-pays* discusses 'presence' at some length, locating it 'within material manifestations of this world' (p. 7).

[5] Bonnefoy, 'À propos de Paul Valéry' (About Paul Valéry) in *L'Inachevable*: *Entretiens sur la poésie* (The Uncompletable: Conversations about Poetry; Paris: Albin Michel, 2010), pp. 100–24; here, p. 121.

dominant realism, its wealth of hyponyms and its tendency to regard the Latinate askance. So the French penchant for the conceptual, the atemporal and a certain 'transparency' versus the English penchant for reality, factuality, pinpointable time and place and 'chewiness' must be tackled at the level of word choice. Then there's Bonnefoy's use of 'literary' words, *hélas* (alas), say, or *ah*! or exclamation marks that contemporary English poetry considers part of a bygone Romanticism, and eschews, unless it deploys them self-mockingly. One can make these disappear—indeed, Bonnefoy himself, in our conversations about these translations, encouraged me to do so if I found them jarring—but should one? Are they not part of his voice, even among his contemporaries in French poetry, many of whom, like those associated with the Oulipo group, are proponents of artificial constraints, and often much more playfully inclined and sceptical of the whole idea of 'depth'. In a 1998 interview with Adolfo Echeverria about his relationship to Mallarmé, Bonnefoy expresses his difference and insists on the necessity of writing about the real conditions of existence, which are 'incarnation in time, in chance, and the desire and the hope that arise from these, in a word, our finitude';[6] he rejects a poetics based purely on relations between words, without any concern for their referents in the outside world.

The last problem is that of translating punctuation; the French generously dispensing commas, even ellipses, where the English pleads for a semicolon or full stop. But if a writer's punctuation is a form of musical notation, one must exercise caution in lengthening the rests or suggesting, syntactically, as the semicolon or

6 Bonnefoy, 'À propos de Stéphane Mallarmé' (About Stéphane Mallarmé) in *L'Inachevable*, pp. 91–9; here, pp. 97–8.

colon do, logical connections where the writer has simply juxta-posed or listed; techniques that can let meanings proliferate where a more scholastic punctuation might reduce the possible meanings to a single one. When I inquired of Bonnefoy how to translate the poem title 'La révolution la nuit', an unpunctuated juxtaposition of two article–noun elements, asking him whether the English title should be 'The Revolution the Night', 'The Revolution, the Night' or 'The Revolution by/at Night', he said he preferred the first (for further elaboration on this question, and others, see my notes, which accompany some of the poems, but which have not been signalled in the text).

I also encountered the more usual problems of French-to-English translation: gendered nouns; the formal and collective *vous* versus the more intimate *tu*—whose absence in English I regretted, particularly when it came to translating the title poem; differences of word order with corresponding changes in emphasis. My tendency, founded partially in a wish to main-tain the flavour of the original and perhaps expand the default solutions of English poetry, has been to keep as close to the original as possible, envisioning difference as opportunity rather than obstacle, while also seeking to retain the collection's lim-pidity and its music, which will necessarily become, in English, a different music: *une lumière* will never be 'a light': not in length, not in sound, probably not even semantically.

*

The final essay in this book, 'In a Piece of Broken Mirror', is not part of the original volume of *The Present Hour.* It is the introduction and title piece in a collection of fifteen short essays written in memory of friends, such as Jorge Luis Borges, Adrienne

Monnier, Gaston Bachelard and Paul de Man, among others.[7] But it also refers constantly, if again fragmentarily, to events and images that are at the heart of *The Present Hour*, and illuminates the poems which, in their own fragmented and unpredictable way, have something of the darting flashes of light caught in a mirror. The essay throws its light not only on the imagery but also on the poetic or creative process that underlies the composition of *The Present Hour*. It shows Bonnefoy deliberately thinking through a piece of writing apparently while he is writing it, as he seeks to discover what lies behind the words; reflecting upon the nature of metaphor, finding it, rejecting it, prodding it, elaborating upon it, accepting a degree of sketchiness, conceding the impossibility of being definitive or even arriving, sometimes, at an acceptable synthesis; and finally, regretting and ruefully accepting the gap (as poems such as 'In a Mirror' and 'The Pianist' also say, metaphorically) between desire and its attainment, or as he says, in part VI of this meditation:

> Poetry is itself an idea. Of all its elans, all its calls, all these convictions mingled with illusions, all these pieces of writing whose purpose is an act of speech, but which soliloquy gets the best of, one must truly think that nothing remains in our lives save instants with no tomorrows, though with hope, nonetheless, which can brighten the colours of many a day.

I am glad that it was possible to include it here.

Beverley Bie Brahic
Paris, December 2012.

---

7 Bonnefoy, *Dans un débris de miroir* (Paris: Galilée, 2006).

THE PRESENT HOUR

STRIKE FURTHER

A Photograph

This photograph—what a paltry thing!
Crude colour disfigures
The mouth, the eyes. Back then
They used colour to mock life.

But I knew the man whose face
Is caught in this mesh. I see him
Climbing down to the boat. Obol
Already in his hand, as if for death.

Let wind rise in the image, driving rain
Drench it, deface it! Show us
Under the colour the stairs streaming water!

Who was he? What were his hopes? I hear
Only his footsteps descending in the night,
Clumsily, no one to give him a hand.

Another Photograph

Who is he, astonished, wondering
Whether he should recognize himself in this picture?
Summer, it seems, and a garden
Where five or six people gather.

And when was it, and where, and after what?
What did these people mean to one another?
Did they even care? Indifferent
As their death already required of them.

But this person, who looks at—this other,
Intimidated all the same! Strange flower
This debris of a photograph!

Being crops up here and there. A weed
Struggling between house fronts and the sidewalk.
And some passers-by, already shadows.

A Memory

He seemed very old, almost a child;
He walked slowly, hand clutching
A remnant of muddied fabric.
Eyes closed, though. Oh—isn't believing

You remember the worst kind of lure,
The hand that takes ours to lead us on?
Still, it struck me he was smiling
When, soon, night enveloped him.

It struck me? No, I must be wrong.
Memory is a broken voice,
We hardly hear it, even from up close.

Yet we listen, and for so long
That sometimes life goes by. And death
Already says no to any metaphor.

I Give You These Lines . . .

I give you these lines, not that your name
Might ever flourish, in this poor soil,
But because trying to remember—
This is cut flowers, which makes some sense.

Some, lost in their dream, say 'a flower',
But it's not knowing how words cut
If they think they denote it in what they name,
Transmuting flower into its idea.

Snipped, the real flower becomes metaphor,
This sap that trickles out is time
Relinquishing what remains of its dream.

Who wants now and then to have visits
Must love the bouquet for its hour.
Only at this price is beauty an offering.

The Missing Name

I

An old man, lying on the ground
In front of the hotel, steps from the beach.
He says he's going to die;
People approach, he turns away.

He says again
That everything should go on as usual
Around him here, in this chance place:
Let the guests come and go,

Waitresses sing as they set the tables
And laugh with the guests.
Still, to the adolescent who kneels down:

'Ah,' he says, 'take this book,
There's a name in it.
Tell me this name that I seek.'

II

This book,
A sheaf of torn pages he clutches.
Two shadows, under mud-splashed glass.
Maybe what's left of a directory.

He loosens his fingers. Leaves fall.
'Gather them up,' he pleads, 'the name is there,
Alas, with all the others.' He repeats,
Yes, that it's in there, that he knew it.

In other worlds
Waves drive the sky against the earth.
Two children walk endlessly down a beach.

He has closed his eyes; he holds out
What's left of the book. 'Tell me,' he says,
'The name that consumes the book.'

III

A name?
Something round and luminous,
Immobile
Like that of Proust's housekeeper.

Yes, yes! Point blank, fire!
Wound him in the shoulder, he's getting up!
Let him twitch, fall back
At peace in the life that will be without end!

I see those two
Talking together. One helps the other
To his feet. They walk off.

The son supports the father, they disappear
Where the quay ends, near the pile of coal.
Their departure—it's strange like the night.

Two Towers

It happened so fast! Imagine!
One tower, and facing it, a second,
And two men, at two windows
Who see each other, first and last time!

And out of anguish, imagine! Out of fear,
Out of desire for justice and the absolute
One brandished a weapon! The other is wounded,
The same flame haloed two faces.

Cease to be hope, which could not
Close the gulf between two towers.
What should have been will not be.

Let the one live; and let the other, in the morning,
Get himself up, collect his tools,
And go off down the tracks, in his silence!

The Garden

Laughing, Pomona stopped and offered you
The shovel, the rake, the sky, the earth,
And the moment, so nothing but sky and earth
Should bend, lovingly, over your dream of you.

The sky cloudy, but just as biddable
The bright showers in her quiet hands.
And maybe a storm: but this evening,
When all shall be well in nothing but life.

The science of a garden is to calm
For an hour the hurt of the wound,
Hortus non conclusus, unbound

By the pump's clatter: when a child
Draws water, in a stone basin,
To scare, in the bottom, a few insects.

The Red Scarf

I

Out at sea a porch in the sky.
Beyond it, the sun. The freighter's captain
Is receiving a voyager.
A porthole is open, waves are lapping.

And what does he do? Gets up, throws
Something out of the porthole, then other things.
Thus: why this scarf, he tells me,
My father gave it to me when I left

On the first of many pointless voyages.
I've loved it, he seemed to be telling me,
I've kept it for this day when I'm dying.

He pushes it out, it flaps back
Over his hand, and swells, then spreads.
Over us a moment, the whole sky is red.

II

That ocean liner, its bridges alight,
That in the night bore down on the small boat,
Could it reverse its course, check
The swell that displaces whatever is,

And silence its music, high in the sky,
And renounce the sign of its smoke?
No, it goes by, it goes off. The boat: left
Reeling in the trough of its wake.

The boat? No, I efface this image
That serves only the dream. No figures
Are carved on the prow of the world.

And what use to him some allegory
Back home that night? Already death
Was taking his hand, was telling him *come*.

The Pianist

I

The keyboard—each morning he returned
To its keys, ever since he thought
He'd heard a sound that might change life:
He would listen, pounding on nothingness.

So a plot of earth once soaked.
The music, now nothing but a glimmer
On a horizon that stayed dark;
He believed lightning was building.

He got old. And the storm shut him
In his house with its panes ablaze.
His hands on the keys mislaid his dream.

Is he dead? Let him get up, in the dark,
Open the door, step out. Not knowing
Whether day is breaking or night falling.

II

A hand ventures, ache of desire,
Into eddies of bright or dark water—
The image shatters; you might think
It no longer has the strength to hold.

And this hand, in a mirror? It comes
Towards his, which comes towards it, the fingers touch
Almost, but in the slight gap yawns
The chasm between what seems and what is.

These fingers, all the same, moving the strings?
Will another hand, from the base of the sounds,
Rise and take them, in order to guide them?

But towards what? I don't know if it's love
Or mirage, and nothing but dream, the words
That have only water or mirror, or sound, to attempt to be.

The Child of the Second Day

The god walking there the first morning,
What might he have hoped from speech?
All he did was assemble stones,
The cairns you see, at crossroads.

Came the second day. And this child appeared
Who, hesitant, picks up a twig
To offer, infinite in his outstretched hand,
To others who, disturbed at their play, fall silent.

They watch him come, they turn their backs,
The raucous sky breaks through the trees,
Its fire strikes, where I heard that laughing.

On the evening of the second day the world ceases,
What might have been will not be,
All night it rains to the roots of the grass.

No God

No god wanted him, or even knew him,
None kept him company in his fatigue.
A dream, this child on the boulevard
Who walks with him, surrounded by light.

None died at the hour of his death,
None reached for his hand in the distraught sheets,
None ever hammered alongside him
At the workbench that took the place of life.

In the words that recount the world, his silence
Wells up, denying them, asking
Me to imagine others, but I can't.

No one bothered to notice him.
What might have been will not be.
Our words don't save; sometimes they dream.

The Revolution the Night

'Father, don't you see I'm burning?' But he,
No, he lets doors bang; the fire ignites
Hallway after hallway of his destiny,
No more doors now, nothing but flames.

And it's true: what use to want so much
But without being able? Having longed to speak,
But without the words to say? Feel regret
But alone: nobody could understand.

Oblivion has covered what little he was;
To me it seemed that he said no to hope,
Wanting only the fire for the dead wood.

Some evenings we'd go walking on the streets.
Down at the end the avenue was red.
But we knew nothing, we didn't speak.

The Idea of a Book

Don't despair! Beside each other,
See, they bend over the same book.
On every page a name is barred,
But the line struck through it, that's the light.

Workman, who wanted in the garden
A little shed, to work in on Sundays,
Come out, into the noonday shade.
Have I this book? No, but you want to think I do.

Come out on the threshold, under the morning glories,
Open your anvil hand towards me.
Come limp with me here into the future!

One rejects memories, alas,
Memory keeps flaring up.
It's a fire one stamps out, not of this world.

Voices on the River

That's the sound of the water! No, listen—
Voices! They're calling us to the river.
How far is it now? We don't know,
It's as if day dawned, through this night.

And you, you don't want me to stop
Looking, listening, seeing, hearing,
You even have words you propose
So that I see further and know more.

I want to, really, I'm not giving up,
But how accept not to have been able
To speak to a desire that had no hope?

What should I have offered he might have liked?
What could I have told him, that made some sense—
The river? Its water knocks at closed doors.

Give Names

She leans over him, she murmurs:
Shall we name some more things
For who knows whether we'll meet again?
Yes, he says, I name you, hesitation

Of the swift about to take flight,
What did it see to make it hover
Briefly in the cry of all the others?
I want to name you so I'll remember.

He turns the page. What he sees
Is that same young woman, smiling,
Back, it seems, from a long voyage.

What is your name for me? she asks
Anxious, sadly. And night falls,
Those swifts, an immense wing on the sky.

The Bed, the Stones

She names the bed, which is vaster
Than the land laid out in front of them,
That confusion of puddles, and rushes,
And puzzled light, and flapping wings.

And he names the stone,
Safre's fissured blocks, broad pools of shadow;
Then each of them names the coming night,
One to call it dark, the other bright.

Let's give two names to the things we love!
Write the world together—that makes sense!
Says anxious Eve to dreamy Adam.

They go, they've named, so far as words permit,
A house, the safre, a hoopoe, a ravine,
A bed, far off, already littered with stones.

In the Mirror

Imagine, placed in a bedroom,
A large mirror. Light from the windows
Catches in it, multiplies. What exists
Becomes what calms. There, outside

It's once again the original place.
Adam and Eve, whose hands meet
Here, in this room, go by.
She, one long skirt, flounced.

I took some fruit; it was in a mirror,
The image wasn't troubled, the summer day
Shivered just a little.

I sensed its colour, its savour, its form,
I set it down, outside. Night came
In the mirror, and the windows bang.

Water and Bread

This scrap of a canvas—torn? Sky
Over a heath where shepherds roam
With nothing, at night, but their cries
To trouble with their beasts the vast dream.

I sense that the painter wanted
The angel who repairs wrongs
To look, even in a painting,
For Hagar and the child who flees with her.

And here they are, and the angel at hand,
But this is where the image is effaced.
The invisible takes back from the colours

The miraculous bread, jug of cool water.
What's left, on the child, is just a glimmer
Letting us dream that in him day breaks.

Low Branches

I

Instant that wants to endure, but how
Wrest eternity from the branches
Protecting the table where light
And shade play on my white page of this morning?

Two trees, and around them the grass,
Then the house, then time, then tomorrow
Opening to oblivion, that already dissipates
Yesterday's fruit fallen close to the table.

Over there is far. Though mostly
Here and now are what's out of reach;
Easier to go into the future

Taking, for later, some pieces
Of this ripe fruit, by whose grace
Blue and green merge in the night of the grass.

II

A single swathe of meadow right to the horizon,
A single thought,
Here names elsewhere in the flight of the cranes,
My only care is to remember

What is present, surging like a wave,
The immense outside reconciled
With what is done and undone
Or wants and unwants, in words.

Come, little girl in your checked dress,
The end of all will be only, laughing,
Words withdrawing over colour.

Wherewith to wrap oneself in the light
Of a summer day in a foreign country,
Hugging to oneself the vocable and its shadow.

BE LOVE AND PSYCHE

I

The hands that sought her in the night
Seemed numberless, she didn't try
To put a face to them. She needed
Not to know, wanting not to be.

Body and soul, to knit your fingers, join your lips,
Do you need the eyes' approval?
Hard-pressed, our eyes, impelled by language
To resist each new enticement!

Psyche was glad that not seeing
Should be like the fire when it drapes
The tree of here in the other worlds of lightning.

Eros, though, longed to keep this face
In his hands; only reluctantly
Did he abandon it to the day's caprices.

II

And all day long is Psyche blind? No,
She pulls up the sheet of the light.
Summer: nothing astir under the sky,
Not even the river in its unmade bed.

She goes, in her body, and alone. But
Who's this stranger pestering, in her blood—
It's as if the spirit desired to be other
Than itself, an embryo at death's breast.

Happy this world where night spills
Into day, and streams in the light.
Wading in this water up to your knees

Is to turn towards another sun,
And the sea's bed is crimson, then one swims
And all is lost that one has been.

III

Drowsy at evening, Psyche likes
Someone else's heart to beat in her body,
All she wants is to be this dark room
Of night's children, sleep and death.

As when one touches a mirror
And fingers come towards our own,
Psyche believes a hand takes hers
To lead her towards more than what is.

Towards more? A flight of stairs descends
And the body tires, hands tighten
On the heavy lamp, knees buckle.

Psyche, why, with your bare shoulder,
Push the door where your future lies?
You enter, you hear that quiet breathing.

IV

And did she light, with trembling hands,
This little flame? Faster than her,
A blot on the image, this peace,
Something black, flung with a shout.

Does Love sleep?—No, his eyes stare,
But they're only empty sockets,
Two holes, with some blood. Is he blind?
Worse, his eyes have been put out.

Large gestures of this large body wakened
By a few drops of burning oil.
You shall go among the world's thorns.

He sits up, he speaks, what does he say?
He draws to his heart the divested,
Hears her shuddering sobs nothing calms.

A VOICE HEARD NEAR A TEMPLE

They are out walking, in the countryside. Countryside? No, not really. Stones, thorn, coarse grass pushing through slabs of grey stone, it's garrigue, nothing has ever been grown here. And no one, either, wandering about this deserted place.

So deserted they are tempted to think they don't know where they've come from.

And here they are in front of some ruined walls, probably what's left of a sheepfold. And—how to resist?—they duck through the door, narrow, overgrown by the branches of a fig tree. Wait, he says. With his hands, he lifts the lowest of these big, gnarled branches and his friend slips underneath. They are in a room. The roof is still intact, ground still covered with stone slabs. The walls . . .

But there are some figures! she calls. Indeed, on one wall, no, on two, on three, men and women, life-size, upright in the crumbling masonry. Oh, effaced! Oh, so little colour remains! You can just make out the red and the blue in the old plaster. As for the faces! How many were there? Only one perhaps. One which has risen, over these bodies that seem naked, like a hot air balloon on the horizon of a summer evening, quickly lost to sight. Are we really sure we see what we think we see? he says, or she says. No, they tell themselves.

But now they are in another room. And there's a pediment, with nothing but an inscription, almost worn away.

Do you think we could decipher these signs, if we tried? asks the young woman, kneeling, almost naked, against the stone, on the reddish gravel where there are some twigs, and pointing to a particular group of letters, six or seven, set a little apart from the rest. No, I don't think so, he responds. They aren't words we would have known, in our lives. He does bend down though. He even kneels in his turn, he stretches out his hand, he too . . . No, let's not try to understand. And besides, it's so dark in here. We are in a temple, she says. We are in a temple's ruins.

They linger. They go from room to room because there are many of them. They walk about as they would have done in their lives. Now with sand underfoot, whose heat they like. And suddenly . . . Oh, what's that? she cries out, fearful. Someone shouted, he replies.

—No, not shouted, called.
—Called, no, it was too . . .

He hesitates, he adds, it was too . . . alone.

And how thick it is, now, this silence that surrounds the temple, that fills these rooms, this high-summer silence with nothing but a few cicadas and a breath of wind stirring in the tiles on what's left of the roof.

—I'm scared, she says.

—No, he says. Maybe we heard nothing.

But then, and as if in response, a second cry, or call, and it's much longer this time, a sort of ululation in which there is complaint, but also something very distant, savage, sad. A few seconds of this modulation, then it ceases. And once more, the huge silence. So—how to express it—untorn. So unpenetrated.

—It was there.

—Yes, right beside us.

They know it's outside, but very close. A few steps outside, to the left of this other door which opens onto some grass, very tall against the light, grass that is tousled, almost blocking the horizon of blue mountains. Grass with yellow flowers.

FRIGHTENED ANIMAL

They struck it accidentally when they were pushing the bushes aside to clear a passage. At eye height up in the branches, caught in them, trapped. They see it, it is watching them. Its gaze is a beating heart, a thought.

And now you take hold of it, extract it from the leaves, it doesn't struggle, would you say its body relaxes, even? As if it knew it was dead already, with one hope left to it, under the bright sky—it's still afternoon—of trying to play at being dead.

Dead, to be left on these stones, endless under their sandals, and over there, in the garrigue, it's already getting dark.

Touch the coat, it's soft. But watch out! The claws!

The coat is the dark brown of a chestnut fallen on the ground, it even has the same patch of white that chestnuts have, underneath. This is also the colour that the side of this hill, which we've been following, is turning. So much for the light that glinted off the gorse a second ago. Brown earth rises under the dark green with its smatterings of yellow and red.

And look at the eyes!

The eyes are the enigma of the world. For is it a gaze, that which you see in this life you hold, wondering what you are going to do with it, yes, set it free, but what else, what first? All the more so as neither of us knows what to call it, what name to give it.

A weasel, a whale, Hamlet said. Or nothing but the drift of the clouds in the sky of this night now fallen. The flageolet has holes our fingers don't know how to stop! A weasel, you say, a ferret? What is a ferret, what is a badger? I would like to know the names, you say. I would like to imagine some, but language is as closed over its gorse and stones as the soil of this hill, right beside us, underfoot even. And I can't even see any more, no, yes, a little bit, these little eyes, this gaze.

And suddenly the creature twists, nearly frees itself. And you tighten your grip, your fingers. It lies still.

Set it down on the stone, over there, ahead of us. That stone which is shining a little, for now the moon has come up, it sends some beams towards this outcrop of rock, a nearly bare expanse of it, and flat, although with bumps. It looks like the altar for a sacrifice.

I touch the animal's back, shouldn't I say goodbye, before it escapes me, in this world that hasn't taught us all the words we need, all the gestures that would deliver us?

And already you are bending down, but we start, both of us, something cried out over there, near the ruins we were in a moment ago. A cry, we listen, what silence, and then it comes again, and lingers, this ululation, then stops.

It's the same one, we tell ourselves. And as by the temple, we are afraid.

But nothing, nothing else in the silence over there and everywhere, this silence which joins with what night is round us, and in us. For it is true, as I said already, that it is night now, except here and there on this small stretch of grey stone, almost shining.

Absent-mindedly you've set the motionless creature down on the stone. And in a single leap it is off, it has disappeared into the dark brush nearby.

TO UNDERSTAND BETTER

Love and Psyche Again

She goes off and one evening returns
To the great castle built over the sea,
Two towers, eyes shut, the sky, the earth
Sleep naked in each other's arms.

Oh, penitent,
You bend over him! Your fingertips graze
His closed lids. You understand
Night and death were merely your dream.

Room after room and him in the last
And cessation of doubt. As if
In your wandering with bloodied feet

You'd stitched up the irreparable.
And your life burrows its head into this shoulder,
And no matter if it's too late and if you die.

At the Garden Gates

Let us dream at the garden gate. Over
The exhausted man and woman
The angel that is death hovers. Neither theology
Nor art to hear them. But look—

They fall asleep, his legs touch hers,
A fire heats their bodies, and what's this
Crawling under cover of the high grass:
A serpent? No, the tree's fruit has split,

The seed has sprouted, and a sort of crab
Has crept forth. Ball of cries
Roughed out of ordinary death.

Painter, make this dream your strategy,
A childhood, and this fire, *pittura chiara*
In the colour of the angel's robe.

Long Red Rays

Explain to me
What those long red rays are, jostling
On the edge of the sky, swelling
Like another future for the light.

My friend, it's the bottom
Of the impenetrable indifference of the night.
The painter mounted these blind eyes,
He spurs them towards us. With his whip

He sets their backs on fire. For painting
Is there any other virtue than the truth?
This painter who doesn't exist yet protects us.

What does he do? He paints a landscape.
Here a little fire, elsewhere night, and for us
This beauty, these hands, outstretched.

He Dismounts

He dismounts, he offers the farewell cup.
He asks where she is going
And why she must. I read this poem by someone else,
I rewrite it, transform it. My friend,

Happiness didn't much smile at me on this earth.
Where am I going? In these mountains
I seek silence, peace of heart. This is my country,
I will not stray far from here now.

My heart? Does it go in peace towards its hour?
See, this earth we love is in flower,
It is spring: the earth is once more as if new,

The peaks of everywhere turn blue again.
Shall I say goodbye? No, may the water
Quicken always, grasses come into bloom.

He Goes Off

In this wash, a sketch for a landscape,
They watched him depart. Uncertain at first,
Then taking this road, then that
And others, still others, into his night.

Those who loved him
Soon saw only the bright remains
Of colour, his red, under this sky
Which hems with the unknown our shores.

Tall trees of over there, thick, impenetrable,
He walks on, immobile, we don't know
Whether he wants to venture into their other world.

Or if, like the sun whose work is done,
He drops his brushes, and goes to stretch out
In peace, on the stone slab of the evening sky.

Beauty

Am I beautiful, O mortals,
Like a dream of stone? No, it's not
This sad assent I want from you.
The child cries on the road, and I forget him.

Am I not beauty
Merely because I flatter your dream? No,
Deep inside me I have eyes wide open,
I crouch, fearful, I am ready

To spring, to claw, to scratch,
Or to play dead if I sense
In your gazes that my cause is lost.

Ask me to be more than the world.
Suffer me to be only this inert body,
Let your hopes, your memories bandage me.

Our Hands in the Water

We stir the water. Our hands seek each other,
Sometimes they touch, broken forms.
Deeper down, a current: some of the invisible,
Other trees, other lights, other dreams.

And see, there are even other colours.
Refraction transfigures the red.
Was it a summer day, no, this is the storm
That will 'change the sky', until evening.

We thrust our hands into language,
They took some words we didn't know
What to do with, being only our desires.

We grew old. This water, our hope.
Others will know how to look deeper
For a new sky, a new earth.

He Reaches the High Seas

He reaches the high seas. I remember
His prow, a face
With closed eyes, smiling. He seemed
Buoyed up, forever, by this mysterious

Movement of the stem, borne along
By dark forces, but desiring a shore
He would not have known, nor wished to say
Where, in the impenetrableness of his night.

The mark of the sword. And this garden
With its forking paths:
Our maps, our portolans in case of doubt.

Ships group at the mouth of the port.
They sail off. Only some lights remain
To mingle with the stars, low on the sky.

A Page from Robert Antelme

I prefer thatch, he would say, to marble,
My little Liré
To words that stray from dream to dream,
Ulysses back home more than at sea.

And they recognized themselves in this voice,
They revived in this recitation
That, faltering, was poetry
And sense, unceasing, and hope.

They couldn't see each other after dark.
But to be it can suffice to hear. Light
Is never so intense as trampled underfoot.

And phoenix was among them. Beating wings
In the barracks. Beak of fire
Dipping sky from the palms of their ashen hands.

The production's only desire, they said, was to conform to the demands of the text.

For example, when the watchmen exchange their first words, the director wanted only to have night appear as the soldiers experience it on the ramparts, in the cold. A cold that pervades the theatre as well, if the place in which they are listening to this can be called a theatre. The spectators, when I arrive, huddle in their clothes, sometimes almost sprawled on the ground, and I have to pick my way through the narrow spaces between their bodies. I see lots of wool coats on the white sand, not so many silk dresses. In fact, it's as if these men, these women—very few children—had arrived days, or, rather, nights ago. Because they've built fires that glow red here and there through the endless darkness. And some of them sleep, I hear quiet, regular breathing, but I also encounter eyes on the lookout, sharp; they frighten me, I hurry on. Sometimes, in the distance, the kind of cries one utters in dreams. I stumble along, double back, keep my eyes on the stage.

The stage? It's vaguely lit, I can just make out some steep rocks, rain and four or five men or women busy round a table with a book on it. One of them picks up the book, looks at the page it is open at. 'I read,' he says, 'Who is there?' Muffled exclamations around him. The director's other great desire is, in fact, to understand the text. Yes, first of all, to take each word literally, but also to ferret out the whole meaning of what they say. How to do this, in this night? The director's assistants, these vague beings crowded round him, don't agree, with him or among themselves, it seems. 'Who is there?' Obviously, how to know who is there?

'And what does it say next?' someone calls. 'Friends to this ground,' answers another. At which a third person bends down, grasps a large stone lying on the ground, strains to lift it, waves his friends aside, tries to throw it, far. 'If the actor throws this stone,' he asks, 'does it mean anything?' 'Careful,' responds a young woman. 'You are one of the actors, don't forget, and the show has already begun.' It has been underway for hours, days.

Suddenly a commotion in the room, people are getting up, stretching, exclaiming, moving about because they've just realized that the play, in fact, is happening elsewhere too, elsewhere as here, for instance, at this very moment, in a chalet up in the mountain along a narrow path where it has snowed in places and puddles still lie on the ground. This chalet, one of those rickety Swiss cuckoo-clock constructions they used to instal upstage in the days of bel canto and the grand old *fin-de-siècle* theatres. You have to push the door, glance into this lit room—a lamp on the table—see Hamlet insulting his mother. Gertrude? Yes, crumpled on a bed, shoulders bare, hair dishevelled. Her hand hides her face. 'Oh Hamlet, speak no more,' she groans. But who cares what happens to her? Now there's a rumour that higher up this same path the director has approached *Hamlet* from another angle. This time, an elegant facade in stone, with stairs leading up to columns, and at the top two indecipherable beings whom I—I, in any case—see silently battling, bare hands against bare hands. How long has this confrontation been going on, how many hours, how many nights will it go on for? Is this 'readiness', this, the sad wish that turns and turns and carves itself a hollow in the chasm of the word? Above this vain combat the rocky promontory, the cold wind.

So many other scenes! And the spectators aware that they must go in search of them, push deep into these sorts of moraines, under the firs crusted with snow, bravely pushing doors from behind which, at times, come rending cries. The theatre is big as the mountain. The theatre is the mountain. Ophelia traipses round, barefoot. We watch her go by, we make space, she is alone, she hums a little, how great her solitude!

What work, this production of *Hamlet*! So many temptations for the director, so many desires to eliminate, but to understand, first of all, to understand! For example, who's this child crying by the roadside? A wise man in travelling clothes, Basho, the benevolent, pauses alongside him, pats his shoulder, asks some questions, listens to him, nods, goes off. And who's this second girl, lightly dressed, feeding big black birds in a kind of stable, where we hear horses stamp, the occasional neigh, in the shadows? They say that in *Hamlet*'s stage directions it's the playwright himself, an actor once more, who is supposed to come towards her, on a long road through the stones of time, the voices of space. He's coming, we don't know where he is exactly, perhaps he's going to turn up somewhere on the vast stage, holding a storm lamp, on his face the mask that is the words of poetry.

HAMLET IN THE MOUNTAINS

They announced that *Hamlet* was being staged in the mountains.

Up there, one was acutely aware that in Shakespeare's mind the prince of Denmark is always surrounded by masses of rocks. Rocks that hang over or crowd round him, faults widening between them, whence it follows that his voice will only ever be heard in the distance, almost always muffled by the roar of water tearing down slopes under the shrieks of rooks from these other worlds.

And the spectators, once they get past the ticket office, a sort of sentry box at the trailhead near the base of a cliff, will have to keep changing place. Why? Is it because the play's scenes have been strewn about, with no regard for chronology, in as many mountain locations? They say some of the original directors expressed a preference for this concept. Some of them wanted Hamlet to insult his mother in a farmhouse up on one of the pastures. By the light of candles that servants would have borne here and there, in one of the rooms, making long shifting shadows on the walls, he would drag her by the hair, throw her on a bed, then collapse in tears at her knees that his frantic hands would have bared. And perhaps in some valley far away from anything, actors are acting, living, growing old in this dire manner in the inexhaustible world, with other scenes taking place elsewhere, ending and beginning again. But others said no, this is not what the mountain wants from Shakespeare.

And indeed! The spectators file across the theatre's narrow threshold, they press forward, all together, endlessly it seems, groping, stumbling, nearly falling into this black night; and over there, up ahead, what is going on? 'Two people are fighting,' shouts a young man who, not without causing much confusion, is running towards me against the flow of the crowd. 'One of them grabbed the other by his collar, he's shaking him, he's shouting.' What does this mean, I want to know, I walk faster, I push through the backs that grudgingly part, under their umbrellas, because it's raining, the cold is also falling from the sky. But my efforts are useless. Upstream, the flux is compact, I am constantly blocked by the trampling and murmuring ahead, I am pushed off onto a side path where, to my astonishment, there is almost no one else.

A few steps on the bright sandy path, puddled with water, and suddenly, two men stride towards me, they go by me, they are talking. I even hear one say to the other, pensively, as they pass: 'What's Hecuba to him, or he to Hecuba?'

And I understand. The scenes of *Hamlet* are not dispersed about the mountain, the actors are dispersed in the crowd. And the scenes are broken up, the action has unravelled, but in the midst of the spectators who stream past, ever more numerous, the great scene nowhere to be found in the work in its simple text will perhaps come together, take shape, shout out its sense even without any of the play's characters nearby.

I can understand this way of thinking. And this desire, I approve of it: all the more in that for the action thus fragmented to have the same degree of density as this trampling which has no more origin and will go on without end, the director, in fact omnipresent, multiplies the number of actors as he sends them off, scattering among the shifting, turbulent flux of this astonished multitude many actors playing Hamlet, many playing Polonius or the startled Gertrude, many Laertes and many Ophelias as well. It follows that these are not just local men and women but as many examples of Hamlet, of Polonius, of Claudius, even as many figures of Rosencrantz and Guildenstern, who, henceforth real beings, more or less, because of the variations of their faces, faces beautiful sometimes, or of the wild gestures which they at times are given, will wander indefinitely in this haggard crowd on the grassy terraces of their immense Elsinore. All of them follow an idea of the self that their representatives serve, and with skill; but all too often they cannot find the words to express this idea. Each is amazed to be what he is, each terrified of these looming rock faces which here allow only the narrowest of passages, but over there seem to open, majestically, on a beyond where torrents endlessly rumble in the bottom of a gorge.

I go on, on a side path, a little above the broadest part of the flood, which by a thousand different ways attempts to carve a path through the mountain, and which here has for the moment been reduced to a trickle of people.

A big man overtakes me laughing.

And now ahead of me, a dozen men, women, stopped. They form a circle, what are they looking at? I slip in among them.

It's Ophelia. She's sitting on a stone, her umbrella at her side, bent over, distraught, groping in some sort of handbag. Scantily dressed, nearly naked, the girl, a poor holey black wool dress as if snatched at by chance upon waking in too big a dream. You can tell she's cold, that her hands shake. Will she draw from her squashed, crumpled bag the fennel, the rosemary, the columbine that the poet wanted her to offer to the world that doesn't listen and doesn't understand? But no, suddenly she gets up and with her head still a little bent, bag and umbrella clutched to her side, throws herself forward, lurching a little. Where is she going? What did she say? Where should I go next?

Hours, hours we are to spend climbing towards this summit which sometimes, at a switchback, lets itself be glimpsed, moonlit, indifferent. Roads fork, many of us have taken them already, others are still hesitating, the wind is still blowing, it won't stop, we know that, even life won't stop: being here is to have to not stop living. Besides, now someone on horseback frays a passage through the people around me, his horse neighs, a black horse, it rears; the actor, is that an actor astride it, is clad in armour, no doubt it's old Hamlet, the dead king.

But why have they draped this red scarf over his coat of mail? True, the wind lifts it very prettily; round this hoary head, it's like the beautiful gestures of youthful writing. And how long it is, this banner, one could believe it endless and that it is already lost among the stars we can still see, God knows why, since it is blowing and raining harder than ever.

THE PRESENT HOUR

I

Look! A flash
Of lightning invades the sky again tonight,
It takes the earth in its hands, but hesitates,
It stands almost still. Did it think

It was a sentence, a signature, no, it flickers,
We watch it fall, illuminating,
In each other's arms,
Sleep and death.

The lightning, an illusion,
Even the lightning.

An illusion, a form
Unfolding, a dream
That embraces form, and is falling
With it, broken,
Dispossessed of itself, over there
On the very edge of our night here,
The present hour.

Look, see.

Look, theologian,
Don't you think God
Has grown tired of being?

You imagine
That being infinite he cannot be done
With himself
But you know that no sacrifice, on his altars,
Not even the sacrifice of his son,
Now awakens any desire in him.

If he turns
Towards the one who slept beside him,
The soul of the world,
If he touches her shoulder, her naked hip,
He will not wake her.

If he goes down
Into his gardens, from terrace to terrace,
Stopping, now and now,
Like those animals
That stand stock-still
For a noise, a shadow,
He will not hear
The sky rustle. Nor the cry
Of despair. Not even
The howl of the slaughtered animal,
Not even
The hesitant piping of a shepherd
Lingering under the last beech tree.

Into thin air
The ox and the donkey
And that lamb, pure astonishment.

The constellations they used to tell us
Sparkled in that straw.

And see, up there, is Venus
Bent over the dying Adonis. And that other image
Is Niobe, all tears. I see Judith
Straighten up, bloody. I see, in the shower of gold,
Danae, her thinning hair. My friend, is it seeing
When the painter has had in his hands
Only bodies whose eyes are closed? I touch you,
Bare shoulders, glimmers in the dark,
Were you the gold shower of a god?

And is your name Ophelia?
You burst out laughing. Your dress opens,
The black water penetrates you, currents
Carry you off. You bend over him,
The mad prince, combing his hair
Matted with fever's sweat, your lips
Brush his temples. The quick water
Muffles his few words, scatters yours.
O betrayed,
Is your name Desdemona?
Willows, willows . . .

And does he name you J. G. F.,
Are you 'his distant Electra'?
Listen carefully:
Illness and death make ashes
Of the fire that flamed for us.

And your name is . . .? No name
For you, of all times
And all places, who fall
With your hands roped in your back,
Your necks broken,
Voices jeered at, mouths
Crammed with earth. No name,
No resurrection for you either.
And no words, not even ours,
Since words baulk
At that which he who tries to say it
Has not experienced, cannot relive.

And what's that on the road there?
It fell from a tree, I pick it up,
The matter lustrous, I have my knife,
I cut into the husk,
I try to nick the woody fruit
But the blade slips. What is
Always refuses itself. Must I toss
Away the kernel with the husk?

Heavy
Under its illuminations of black sky,
The page of the book. One would like to pry
Even a corner up, see beyond
Into the space of other pages. But the pages
Are stuck, they wad. They seem glued
By a water of the end of the world. Peat
Good for one last fire? Must we think

The sign that caught the flank of things
Like lightning, and made a spark there
Was nothing but hands joined in vain,
Dreams, fitfulness of merely dreams,
A mummy all dolled up for nothing, under its stone lid?

Night falls. In the bedrooms
The bodies are naked. Now a movement
For no reason, incomplete,
Shakes a sleeper tormented by his dream.
Shall I touch this shoulder, this one,
Plead with eyes to open, open wide,
Bodies to resuscitate, as we once believed
Occurred? Shout,
Come back, Claude, come back, Enzo, from the dead?
I shout names, no one wakes.

And so entangled our words
With one another! Come apart—they don't.
Do they sleep
Folded in each other's arms? Nothing seems
To pulse in the arteries I touch
In the hollows of their shoulders. I think of the day
When, in the astonishment
Of sky and earth approaching
each other, mingling,
Becoming the horizon, then the road,
Stick rubbed stick and turned to fire.

And now one of us shudders, rolls over
On his bed, he takes his eyes

Off his chimera. But the mirror
Sleeping at his side doesn't wake.
Does it reflect the cypress, the stars,
The lovely face of the young woman
Asleep on the warmth of her bent arm?
No, if I take the mirror from the wall
And hold it up to the things of dawn,
What I hold is a lump of coal,
The reflections stir in it only night.

II

I have gathered the fruit, I open its husk.
In our words
The quick drift of the cloud.

Illusion,
The hearth that burnt bright each evening, remember,
In the house we loved.
The kindling,
The paper crumpled up, the poker,
The sudden flame, almost like lightning,
A dream, like us?

And remember
The poisoned dog! Its yelps clawed
The sky, the earth. My friend,
Again yesterday
We walked all the way to those gates, over there,
Through the dips where water shines in the grass.

Yesterday, we walked past
The empty barn. Tawny, an owlet
Flew from the eaves. I call its name,
Nothing moves on the moonlit wall.
No eyes of a frightened creature.

Illusion, the almond tree, all its bloom
Like fires among other stars.
Dream, smoke,
The skies of those nights, all those clusters?
The lamb? Only ever
The knife and the blood. Our ravine,
Nothing but water whose voice growls
At times, then dwindles to a thread.
No one
In the torrent's roar. No one
In the light. That man
There, with his brain of gold,
Who staggers along the sidewalk, his bloody fingers
Clawing at the mind's shreds,
What did he offer, which bouquet? I want those flowers,
To lift them from their wrapping,
The reddened page, for I perceive,
In the gift he, already dying, made
The abysses of sky and earth,
The images that clouds make
And corollas, the man, the woman,
Whose colour seems to stay bright,
But all of that—flung into the gutter,

He threw away the rejected offering,
Won't I be picking up only the wilted,
Senselessness, an acrid smell, insipid?
Roses, roses? Only torn
Roses exist, no rose in itself,
No corolla to build a world.

III

And yet, I can say
The word *chevêche* or the word safre or the word *ciel*
Or the word *espérance*,
And glancing up I see those trees along the road
Set on fire by an evening sun.
It is a very gentle fire, its bright embers
Transmuting foliage into light,
And here, there's the field, over there some peaks,
And their hands meet, their bodies seek each other
With this silent evidence
That surely we must call beauty.
I look at the trees for a whole hour,
Is that the visible: barely, since
Visibility is changed to pure gold—
Yet all around us the night falls.

I listen to a word, I try to see what it designates,
And it seems to me, irrepressibly,
That this thing regains its colours, that eyes
Open once more, astonished,

In the mind's dream of stone.
Do the words hold more than we ourselves do,
Do they know more than we do, do they seek
At the edge of some water, black and rapid,
That we from the depths of our sleep refuse,
The stepping stone of a light? And this light,
Has it a sense, in a completely different way,
Of course, than yesterday's hope?
I listen to a word, set it beside another,
This sleeper and this other sleeper wake
In a patch of sun, their hands touch,
Is this merely desire,
The same dream despite its new visage?
The lightning that pierces in vain the sky of here?

But veridical is the landscape painting,
Veridical the broom
Flowering in the desert,
Veridical the voice that named it
In our exterminating words, on some sad slopes.
And see, on the road,
Those two walking.
They stop, suddenly,
Turn towards each other. Do they argue,
Insult each other, will they tear into each other, out of anguish
At being the illusion they know they are?
No, they seem to be looking at the evening sky,
Where an infant sun appears, its huge head
Already high on the old horizon.

And it's true that the trees I saw
Become incandescence, continue,
Not far from them, to be that ray of light
Come from we know not where, effaced only
By refining, in its last moments,
The grains of a gold one would say immaterial.

Look at me,
Say what rises in them from language's depths,
Forget who you are so that I may be,
Make of me what I seek to be,
Renounce your dream for mine,
Love me, give me form, countenance
With your hands of shadow and light. The evening sky
Is, perhaps, a rose. Rose to come
Through your horticultural work in the clouds,
Rose of trees, of rivers, of roads,
Of unmade beds, of simple hands, seeking
Other hands, blindly. Rose of words
One person says to another, through nothing yet
But a tingling in the palm, in the fingers.
The sky changes. The rose without why
Is you, in the gardens of its colours.
Look, listen! The least word
Has in its depths a music,
The phoneme is corolla, the voice—it is the being
That can flower, even in what is not.

And late, taking pity
On the images. See how Danae

Rises on her couch, though she knows
The god is illusory. And Ophelia
Bears away in her eyes, like a certitude,
Sky and earth, though their twin fires
Drown in her utter night.
Ahead of us, my friends, is that evening
Or a sort of dawn without form? Sun,
All the same, deep in those red glairs.

You look at the sky
Through the open window, a child
Of this impoverished century. The world,
These grey tin roofs, curls of smoke,
This soiled, torn page? No, your words
Refuse to be effaced from the universe;
Of this nothingness they want to make hills,
Roads, valleys. Aren't those mountains
Only stone and snow, no, at the summit
Of one, not too high,
A meadow lies. And utterly peaceful
Seems, from here,
The shadow that flits over the green
Of its endless grass. Further down, the river
Gathering, shining. Will you be able
To hope that this evidence has meaning,
That it will affirm itself in your words,
That it may be the magnet that will draw
Spirit back from despair; are you going to think
That there is being only in images but that this

Suffices as mystery, inasmuch as
This nothingness consents to the light—
Indifferent, uncreated—by the gestures
Of its contours, its shifts, of the laughter
In the depths of its tragic voice carrying
Towards others some of these shadows? Perhaps not.
All at once the sky darkens, lightning falls.

But you turn
Towards your rented room in this suburb,
It is small, but its walls are almost white,
And on them you've placed, this first day,
Diana and her Companions, by Vermeer,
Just a photograph but of an exchange
Of such mildness, with hands so pure
That the group of figures stands out
Against the grey and black of the absent colour
Not like the sun but better and more.
A dream is a falsehood. But dreaming, no.
Let your dreams be
Two fighters, one masked, but now and then
Rich in his discovered face.

You watch the evening live. The sky, the earth
Naked, reclining, on their common bed.
And he, clouds, simply clouds,
Leans over her, takes in his hands
Her respected face.
God? No, better than that. The voice
That goes, breathless, to greet another

And laughing desires her desire,
Anxious to give more than to take.
Aren't you going to think, this evening again,
That matter, spirit, can become
The same breath? That from their calm,
Restful embrace
Some colour, some gold may fall,
Some shard of glass, mud-splashed,
But shining, in the grass?

And death, as usual? And having been
Only images each for the other, stirring up
Embers, in nothing but our memories, yes, I agree,
But remember
Childhood's meadows: remember walking
On the way to lie down and look at the sky
Charged with so many signs but immense
Within you this benevolence,
Flashes of heat lightning of summer nights.
Present hour, do not renounce,
Take back your words from the lightning's errant hands,
Listen to them making of nothing speech,
Risk, risk
Even the confidence that nothing can prove,

Will us not to die despairing.

AUTUMN SHIVERS

Where are we going to put this mirror?

Nowhere! Let it sit on this table, reflecting only the sky, and for no one.

The sky? Not only the sky, also a corner of the archway, with its wide moulding from another century. Outside, through a window we made in the wall, the garden, what would have been the garden. And at night, if we bend over the mirror, we'll see a vague gleam of stars above the trees.

And where's this chromolithograph going to go? We bought it, not without some perplexity, you recall, at the annual rummage sale in the next village. Hard to see what it is under the tarnished glass!

Hard! Don't you see? It's a lake in front of mountains, a small boat. And aboard it, two young women in pink dresses, with big hats, veils and bouquets of flowers in their hands. The water is clear but night is falling. And another boat bobbing a little further on, with musicians, a singer. What a voice! These veils, I remember them, people wore them when I was a child, to look stylish! But mourning veils often, black gauze.

The hall door is banging, do you know why?

I don't know.

And that walking up in the attic? It's the same bird as every evening. Now is when it wakes up. I'm going up there. I can watch it fly off for the night through the open window.

Don't go!

There's nothing to be afraid of! Listen rather to how loudly the young man over there on the water is singing. Too bad, now there's some mist. He's rowing his boat towards the other boat, but all we see of him is a red spot dwindling into the mountain's shadow.

I've heard they make fires on boats, up in those mountains. That the boats drift across the lake, late into the night.

Let's go see, let's gaze off into the distance since our house doesn't exist.

TALL SHADOWS

Remarkable, the art of this very ancient folk whose works we contemplate in these rooms, whether of caverns or museums we don't know. They are, clearly, shapes of men and women but whose arms are excessively elongated and hang down their sides or reach upwards and whose hands also seem stretched out, dilated, moving; to say nothing of the heads, some of which seem to be crowned with the great antlers one sees on deer when they grow old. And everything within these figures, within their strange outlines, the same dark-blue colour.

Don't be surprised, I am told: these worshippers of the setting sun were interested only in the shadows that lengthened ahead of them on the fine sand of their beaches or on the grass of their meadows. They would gather in the evening, as the sun was sinking, soon it would be almost touching the horizon; and, facing east where the same sun, so they hoped, would reappear, they watched their shadows lengthen ahead of them, much longer now than they themselves are tall. Their desire? To exchange signs by waving their arms or hands at the stormy-looking crests of these bodily extensions; and, in brief, over there, to speak to each other better than here, extending towards others' shadows some part of their own, for example, the fingers, sometimes splayed, which became, as the sun went down, fantastic: a bird whose wing touched, oh, delicately, modestly, a shoulder, or even the nape of a neck. Their life? It was over there, yes, over there, at the edges of the light glowing redder and redder, at the edge of the peaceful sky and earth, that it was acted out: not here, where they paid little attention to their day-to-day life, getting things done because one has to but often raising their eyes from their work of the moment to look at one another, to exchange complicit smiles. So the hours passed, the sky changed, soon it would be time to leave the fields, to come out of the houses with their veiled mirrors, walk beyond the last big trees of the road, in order to continue side by side right to the open space and, there, try to tell one another, at a good distance, all the beautiful things they had thought about during the day.

For, I am told again, they were a happy people. The urge to discuss, to dispute, the annoyances, the jealousies, had they felt the need to be expressed, to become conscious thought, would have rapidly evaporated into what was light, gentle, dance-like, the zigzag of the shadow at the end of arms lifted overhead or turned towards consenting or shyly hiding bodies; or at times metamorphosed into movements not easy to understand, out of a desire, it seemed, to reach this or that rock sticking out of the grass, very far away all the same, to graze it, touch it. Touch it? Maybe even grasp it, shadow, shadow's fruit that this rock too had become, in the hollows of the falling night?—not necessarily, in truth. An observer, had there been one in those days and in those lands, might have seen in one or another of these gestures something other than the happy anxiety of a contact which is almost established, is lost, will nonetheless occur: pleasure of the game, delight in the self, the happiness of an existence that grows aware of another, in the light. He would have perceived at such times, in fact quite rare, a fluttering, a feverishness, a haste to possess the other shadow that might signify the fear of a small disappointment, even a moment of sadness, when the desiring hand would be united with desire's object but scarcely more than in image.

Metaphysical, certainly, this concern; and in great danger of theological speculation these men and these women who really only came alive when night was about to fall. In the first place, by thinking in this way only of the evening sun, it was necessary that during the whole day they remain silent, exchanging words only so that life might go on without too much care and fatigue. Then there were the children who, astonishingly, didn't understand these departures at the end of the afternoons. Not that they didn't enjoy them, they too played with their shadows, when they came to the vast rim. They fluttered their arms, they skipped, they laughed. But they ran everywhere, hiding behind their parents, having fun enlarging the shadows of their parents who cared not a whit about the small lives entangled in their legs; they exclaimed, they shouted. They got tired, as well, went off to sit down somewhere, wanted to be carried on the road back, only thinking now about the meal they would have in front of the fireplace whose flames made shadows dance on the kitchen flagstones.

Are the children out of place and too much perhaps in a poetics of shadows? Other observers wondered if these shadow worshippers weren't motivated by an idea of the theatre. By the feeling that over there, between the earth and the sky, in the debate between the still sunny grass and these silhouettes already a little aware of night, a drama was perhaps beginning to take shape—to acquire meaning—which could never be explicated here, among us, its actions escaping the categories of language. These observers—these critics—imagine that the participants in these games, rites, in fact, will speak to one another, all the same, once night has come, back at the house, even maybe once the fire is out or at least has been reduced to nothing but embers in the dark hearth with, now and then, a flame or two flaring up. They huddle, in the dimness of bedrooms, they hold hands, they laugh, some of them, briefly; they evoke, in an undertone, God knows what event that one of them might have believed he saw sketched on the high boards of their evening's stage. And they try to understand it, this event, they are touched by it, they hope. Alas, there are also, in the sleep that overtakes them, voices that incite them to despair.

What do they wonder about? If, among their shadows over there, an extra shadow hadn't slipped in, that day, but yesterday too, and perhaps at other times as well? A shadow that resembled them, the same hands widening at the end of the same distended body, but no, it was neither you, nor me, nor him, nor her, and besides it had only been there for an instant, this something more, perhaps man, perhaps woman, perhaps, who knows, mysterious beast, Cervidae. An instant, only an instant? But time, the sun going down, didn't it hesitate, don't you think, you and you, as if it were reflecting, splashing in those puddles of shadows and lights, imagining—what new skies, what new horizons!—halting its trajectory? Illusion, yes, distant mirages, these fleeting impressions. But if, tomorrow, this instant came back and, this time . . .? One talks about this, the hours of night rush towards the estuary of dawn, the sun is going to rise, day begin again. Art—vast scenes in appearance all serenity—is being born in one of these houses, the one whose hearth doesn't stop, for some reason, casting shadows of beasts and children on the bright flagstones.

GO, KEEP GOING

I

And now we are at sea, my friends, in a small boat the waves lift then let drop again, but which persists, almost on end at times, courageous!

And to the left and right and also ahead, where the sea ought to be free, we must steer clear of ships, their high sides sometimes so close to each other it's a miracle we aren't crushed and are making headway!

Almost a closed room this body of water that zigzags between and slaps against their unlit sides! And we are anxious, one of us at the helm, the others bent to the oars, but also we glimpse the figureheads that tower over us. Goddesses with long supple shoulders, bare breasts, arms and hands whose deep blues, ochres, crimsons are flaking off. Mothers smiling, though with eyes closed, though sad.

One last effort, my friends! One of us rises from his bench, hands cupped round his mouth, he's going to direct the manoeuvre. Soon we'll be out of here, free!

II

For yes, my friends, we have to get through this brush, over here, this way! Come on, let's plunge in, up to our necks in these branches, among brambles, it's not so dense as it looks, nor so deep, we've only a few dozen yards to push through, heads down, arms across our eyes, our cheeks scratched but not too much, and see: already there's light on the ground, under our feet.

Underfoot? Yes, phosphorescent, stones under our almost bare feet, smooth stones, elongated and round, in different colours under this tangled mess of vegetation. And which each instant become more numerous, overlap, slip and slide and we slide with them, falling: but right away we pull ourselves up, don't we, and we go on, we go on! Oh, these stones, with night falling, true heaps of them now, they form pyramids, countless, shadowless rays escaping from them.

III

And words, all that, words, for in truth, best of friends, what else do we have? Words that shrivel under our pens, like insects we kill en masse, big splintery words, that scrape us, words that flame up, suddenly, and we have to extinguish this fire with our bare hands, it's not easy.

Words whose tangles dissimulate holes, into which we slip and slide, shouting, but it doesn't matter, our life, so little thought goes into it, don't you think! Quick, we get a grip on ourselves, we begin to speak again.

And I did tell you, didn't I, my handful of companions, I did tell you that day is breaking? Come on, let's keeping going, gather all our wishes, all our memories, you those shouts, those calls, those howls, those sobs, and I, too, this laughter, these great howls of laughter everywhere so far away under this sky so low we can touch it with our out-stretched hands! It is clear that day is dawning, my friends, clear it breaks over us, colours everything once more, takes away and disperses everything.

IN A PIECE OF BROKEN MIRROR

I

I bring together these evocations of men and women who are no longer alive and I look for the signifier, maybe the metaphor, that could somewhat convey—or even explain—how I feel about these pages: that they are only allusive, not at all central to a reflection that wants to say or discover more. I see that I took pleasure in their gaps, in their sketchiness, and it comes to me that this is because of the way light and shadows play over these pages, in these words, in which memories get caught.

What is this light, what are these shadows? I might tell myself that death is a curtain that one, all of a sudden, draws over oneself; and for the person who bends down to the face that is sinking, the light is transformed, momentarily, into mystery itself. But it is not these shadows from below and off into the infinite—opaque aqueous shadows—that I have in mind, it seems to me; those I glimpse on the occasion of writing these brief pieces feel weightless to me, I imagine them almost dancing, offering themselves to, rather than refusing the light's embrace. Movements whose grace I really wish I could restitute, in these people whose lives I have known, elans which however are sometimes brusque and which go off and break against the nearest wall. Except then, it also seems to me that they bounce back, intact, full of life.

There is surely something in these fleeting but recurrent impressions that the pieces of writing, often born of circumstance, couldn't say or even try to say, being each time restricted in scope and scarcely broader in ambition. It's as if I found again in each of them, today, some desire forever frustrated; only my memories of Michel Rossier allow me perhaps to feel that I have responded in some degree to what the circumstances required: but again, without knowing how.

II

So I must think some more and begin by remembering that in my mind I have long associated my wish to collect these brief pieces of writing, to which I'd grown attached, with the idea of mirrors. As if I had pretended, to myself, that they fulfil the promise of this sort of task: to be faithful, and rich in the precise and numerous details such as a mirror procures.

Portraits in a mirror, these evocations of Jean Wahl, say, or of Diana Fiori or of André du Bouchet? Faithful reflections, in the mirror that, it turns out, will have been me? Definitely not. I am utterly incapable of the psychologist's informed gaze or the memorialist's or the historian's probing one, and so much the better, in one way, for the data gathered by such approaches has a tendency to find itself shut out of whatever it is they seek, like the mirror—the plane-surfaced mirror—with its vain exhaustiveness. True, I've not forgotten that Alberto Giacometti dreamt that literality was the best approach towards rendering the model, and he wished to push this method very far, he wanted it absolute, but, in fact, in his work he kept discovering that this quest was, each time, a cul-de-sac at whose far end, off over there under a basement window, in a cellar light, someone is only perceptible by a cry that seems to be a cry of anguish.

Not all mirrors are flat, of course. And are we not, each of us, convex mirrors of the sort the French call 'witches' mirrors', whose convexity so distorts the person looking into them that it makes little sense to note the figure's multiple aspects, even if these are still present under the distortions? What is most distorted in such mirrors is what is closest. And what governs in such instances are the equations proper to optical instruments: the mirror's curved surface inflects by the operations of an irresistible geometry the rays of light that the object emits. We too, each of us, have our personal equations. We too, with a force equal to that of curved mirrors, distort whatever outside reality has of appearance or significance.

So be it, but it gives me no joy to see myself as this sort of mirror. I am not even quite prepared to think that my gaze at these beings, about whom I have written out of affection for who they were, should be subject to my law as completely as such a device is. Are the constraints born of the language that I have constructed for myself, that I speak, really as implacable as those of matter? I cannot resign myself to think so, which leads me to wonder if there isn't something more behind this mirror idea, why it keeps coming back. Is it simply a metaphor's suggestiveness, or does it hide old memories that want to return to life?

III

And indeed, I have many memories of mirrors that evoke for me something quite different and more than the strict *données* of optical science. In many cases, I perceive in mirrors my attraction for what we call their water, a depth and limpidity they owe not to the simple effect of a blind law but to their matter: the glass or crystal of their reflecting surface and the reflective coating of mercury or tin applied underneath. Causes hard to quantify but nonetheless at work in the often gracious welcome such mirrors extend to the person who comes up to them.

It may happen that the water of one of these mirrors is so pure one could say it is invisible, but even so, it hasn't been completely effaced through the workings of optics, for a very thin haze of colour, risen from the silvering, tempers the transparency. And looking into this water one encounters something very different from the hard exteriority that mere geometric reflection retains of the object. Here, one stands on the threshold of a depth whose figures are now less facts of space than beings in a beautiful light, and who speak of it to us. Is the light, they ask us from where they stand over there in the image, truly the extremity on whose edge all form will be effaced, hence proof of our non-being? Is it not rather the first step to another level of reality, the ray of light from a Garden of Eden to which we might return? Our gazes, our desires plunge into the water of these lovely mirrors. They dream of a plenitude of being that life refuses us.

Now it also happens, more often than not, that over the years, or even centuries, the mirror's water grows troubled; one encounters shadows, shoals of mist, even rust spots and moirés: so that it is no longer in an immediate and immediately complete manner that the image is perceptible in them; one has to seek it out among eddies or iridescences often difficult to ford. And as this search can only be undertaken with the necessarily subjective consciousness one has of the world, it arouses the most personal desires, with the imagination as guide, and seems for this reason a path towards the truth.

So in Mallarmé's 'Winter Shiver' that reverie among others. The poor and solitary young man who writes this poem owns one of those mirrors whose silvering has, no doubt, for a long time been somewhat altered whereas its frame carved with perhaps smiling figures seems to make of the mirror a doorway into another world and another life. And he who speaks on this page turns towards his companion, who is herself hardly visible in the light of late afternoon, with a question and an invitation. 'And your Venetian mirror, deep as a cold fountain, rimmed with gilded guivres, who is reflected in it? Ah! I am sure that more than one woman has bathed the sin of her beauty in this water; and perhaps if I kept looking, I would glimpse a naked ghost.'

Such mirrors are far less what repeats the world than what incites us to replace it with our dream. I have experienced their power to carry me away, and how this can be especially potent in places where we have already yielded to some illusion or other. One such place? For me, for us, this was a landscape where for thousands of years roads had been maintained, with fields and barns, wells and cisterns, here and there, but which now was becoming deserted, with great boulders that frost and winds had sometimes worn more or less spherical.

And here is one such cistern, off in the distance of an afternoon only just beginning to decline, all but immobile. The cistern's top is closed with a sheet of tin, the two halves separated by a rusty hinge. We lifted it up, it clattered back into the stillness. We bent over: two or three metres below, a little water shines, but with weeds and other obscure small lives pocking its surface, as if to keep the sky's reflection at a distance.

I evoke this cistern because, for the couple who, shoulders touching, laughing, looked down at this half-clear half-murky water, the real place was then so satisfying, in this corner of the world, in this endless season, that the light glimpsed beneath their own two reflections in the water, a light all the more convincing as it was somehow denied by the layer of shadow, appeared the same to them as that which prevailed around them at the dawn of their nights, and was proof that reality acquiesced in their dream, whereas they ought already to have understood that it was the surrounding countryside and that house over there and their present life that was the illusion they should shake off.

The light in mirrors gives nothing of the sort to the person who turns hopefully towards what, in its make-believe depth, is not light but only its reflection one more time, be it the last one, and this light is therefore the worst sort of enticement. As reflection it has become an image as much as any thing or any existence is when it lets itself be caught in a mirror: the light encourages us to remain in the Garden of Eden of images, to believe in the illusions from which images are born, making us like Midas, destined to solitude by his attachment to the gleam of a gold that is merely a dream. And it is not the aged silvering of mirrors that lets us vanquish this misapprehension of the other, and of the self, turned into metaphors by the optical effects of mirrors: quite the contrary. Those old mirrors do not justify my going on trying to make sense of this word, so insistent, *mirror*.

IV

But I have other memories, I know. And writing about them may tell me whether thinking about mirrors is or isn't a wrong road.

Memories, or dreams of memories? But all memories are dreams and certain moments of our lives have, at the time of their occurrence, been so invaded by dreams that to remember them is to reveal the essence of our past but also of our desire, of our future.

I think, for instance, of something I used to love doing when I was what one calls a child, a word whose meaning, as I am increasingly aware, is rather uncertain: I loved to carefully smooth out those pieces of silver paper that candied chestnuts or chocolate come wrapped in, finishing the job off with the back of a table knife. Did I want to see myself in this cramped surface?

I think of this game, if it was a game, and I wonder if there wasn't already a hint in it of my current preoccupation. What, in fact, happens in this other sort of depth? As completely smoothed out as it may be, the tin or aluminum foil keeps traces of its folds, there are creases, and for this reason the image that appears there is somewhat vague, out of focus, which could remind us of what happens with reflections in mirrors whose silvering has deteriorated. So is the image here, as elsewhere, an incentive to dream? And is the pleasure of little by little bringing out the image that of slipping into a dream?

I think not, and I come to understand that my concern about dreaming was in fact at the root of my absorption in those bright squares of foil. For under the resemblance of the two images is a difference that gives pause. In true mirrors what troubles the image? Alterations in the silvering, flaws in the glass; and beneath these wisps of shadow and other spots or patches of rust, one nonetheless perceives reflections with as much clarity of form and colour as the directly perceived aspect of whatever they reflect and repeat. Over there in the image the slightest details of the sensorial data remain accessible to the gaze with all the infiniteness offered to sensible beings as occasions for reverie.

Now, nothing of the kind in the scrap of foil. The trouble this time is not on this side of the reflection but at the heart of the reflection itself, like a slight imprecision in the rendering of each detail. This affects everything in the image, what is off in the distance as well as what is right up close, so that it is the light itself, the only other element of our experience at this minute, that seems to effect the change in our perceptions. We might think that there are cases when the light doesn't have, or doesn't want to have, its usual and supposedly natural capacity of penetration. We might even ask ourselves if, in reality—this reality, the being what it is that this small device reveals—the light doesn't lose interest in the outsides of the things as they are presented to us by optics' unintuitive laws. In a word: we imagine that the light renounces what is merely visible out of a prescience—who knows?—of an invisible.

What's more, look how at the finger's slightest movement the image leaps off the paper, bounding who knows where. There's no time for narcissistic reverie, busy as we are trying to immobilize this reflection and grasp the sense of its movements. If indeed it was us, who appeared there, for a moment, must we not conclude that we appear and disappear in the world in a manner just as brusque and unpredictable as this brief reflection: this world being even, as in this shadow of an image, a simple background with neither stability nor duration? A completely different thought, that of the being or non-being of our very lives, perhaps merely appearance, takes the place of the dreams of real life that proliferate in mirrors.

Mirrors flatter our illusions. But this other occasion of metaphysical disquiet, the piece of smoothed-out silver paper, in which one tries to see oneself, gives us to understand that we live among nothing but illusions, and merely as one of them, leaving us with the presentiment, however, that the light is capable of turning away from this fallacious exterior of things to which mirrors limit it, and perhaps this has meaning for us, who are at loss in the world. We begin to tell ourselves: doesn't light have powers that only in appearance—that's the right word—deny the optics that trap it in their too-precise-to-be-true reflections and refractions? And can't we help light escape from mirrors, which would at the same time be an escape from ourselves?

Not only silver paper suggests such thoughts. Let the wind come up, let a French door start banging at the threshold of a garden, tossing a ray of light between the trees outside and the darkened room, making a hole in the reflection one might have glimpsed in the windowpanes, and the same vast question grips us, this door that bangs is one of those absolute events and the chance we must seize.

V

And the sheds! I see myself, and this is yet another very real memory, in one of those sheds built at the bottom of gardens in small cities or villages. Into these lean-tos one crams the things the house has no room for, chests, drawers yawning open, carelessly rolled-up carpets, chipped odds and ends of bric-a-brac and even, behind the coiled garden hose or chicken wire, a few good-sized old photographs touched up with sepia or garish colours: portraits of grandparents or of great-uncles or vaguely smiling but nonetheless doleful aunts.

And alongside such often rather heavy frames there may well be mirrors too, their top corners rounded as if to suggest that they are thresholds, not merely things. Mirrors no longer wanted in the bathroom or above the fireplace, whose clock has also been dispensed with.

And what is truly remarkable is that during the day one scarcely thinks about these sheds, so full of things that, in truth, one can no longer squeeze into them; but let night fall and the child of the house thinks of them, hears the call, ventures in, sidles between the upended table and the sacks of plaster, goes over to the portraits and mirrors that wait, propped against a wall. Why? Because in this dark place, when the moon is up, some light flashes off the glass. A surface light, not from the depths, the silvering of this mirror being only the obscure disorder of the place, boards piled up, cobwebs, shadows of images and the greyish cement down at the bottom. Whence it follows that if one lifts a corner of these more or less heavy frames, to begin to move them, the water which is common to them remains still, there where it is, outside the world, black, while the light which had flickered on the glass moves, becomes a ray that darts left or right or up or down, even projecting at times a vague shape on the nearest wall. What is one doing, trying to shift these objects, with clumsy gestures? Perhaps to make of this awkwardness the presentiment of contradictions or inhibitions one will experience in the life to come.

Many years later, that big mirror we brought down from the upstairs bedroom when we had to give up our house of some years; and which, night falling already, was left outside for a while against a wall on the slope towards the ravine. I imagined it was going to spend the night out there and that dew or a little rain would stick to it, so that the light of the sky would not only touch it without penetrating it but would, prismatically, be multiplied by the surface drops; under which, it's true, the other water that aggravates dreams would still be there watching. I imagined the light set free some time during the night. Disentangled from our aspirations and dreams and pouring over this lost house, over these beings who are giving it up, the same gold of indifference and peace as that which exists among star clusters.

But what a vain thought! It's only oneself one can expect to make things happen between light and mirror.

VI

How to set the light free? How to help it escape from a mirror, how to free ourselves from ourselves?

In fact, I know. All I need is to think about my pleasure the time I caught sight of a piece of broken mirror in the grass, in front of the old house, lying there who knows how long, a long ago we'll never know anything about. Yes, look, it's a piece of broken mirror, that thing glinting over there, half-buried! Let me pull it out, grab hold of it, carefully wipe off the damp earth.

Why such pleasure? Because we were outside, in the sun, some shadows, and the whole big sky in front of us; and rays of light darted from this piece of glass when I moved it, as if it had a wonderful, impatient desire looking for a way out.

And why not hold it so that the beam of light alights on this face close to me, on the eyes, for fun, a little annoyed, all the same; the eyes close, they reopen, the arc of light flits off, threatens to return, pretends even. And look, there it is, back again, and over there, at the edge of where it gleams in the faint half-light—is that only a face, whose features one thinks one understands, but in thinking this one is already making up the past? No, that's—how to say this—a being: present in her reaction which is her relationship with another being, and her future with him.

Delusions of distances which then come undone in the truth of the near! Consumption of space, with its vain optics, in the truth of the instant! Round us, the heat of summer, heat's silence, time's precious remainder evaporating off the stones: life itself, since it is now shared. I think of such moments and tell myself that light really does escape from mirrors. Other such moments and we'd be free, wouldn't we? Free to give and receive, to consent, to make alliances, all the unhoped for, never renounced. Yes, but what to do, after having played, for a moment, with this mirror shard? One sets it down on the terrace's parapet, leaves it to reflect for nothing the depths of the empty sky.

I am not the person to hold on to a piece of broken mirror found in the grass.

But having found a place for this memory, I know better what it was I had in mind and only partly understood each time I have had occasion, often a volume in homage to or in celebration of an anniversary, to recall a friend, someone close but no longer alive; and why, gathering these writings in which I have sought to do so, I have come to see darting about in them something like a reflection of a reflection, like the shadow of a dancing light.

Let those friends be no longer here; isn't what remains regret for the encounter that didn't occur, which would have allowed—through its unforeseenness, through some lucky chance, as we say—a more essential sharing than that experienced? The sharing of simple hours on the sort of roads the hand of friendship offers, the sharing of thoughts that can be livelier when reciprocity of attention takes the place of meditations that are merely monologues? Behind these occasions, often missed by so little, lie the shapes of other sorts of encounters, during which the most difficult and secret sides of oneself might be revealed, resolved. Yes, this is the regret that assails us and it is this that the play of shadow and light signifies, rather, aggravates, since it shows us, in the uncertain nature of its occurrence, exactly what small piece of mirror one has at times left lying, here or there, in a sadly distracted manner and, therefore, what future is lost in such moments of life.

What to do now? One tries to remember, one remembers haphazardly, and besides, it's too late, true as it is that one can only note that the little light with which one could have engaged in life's most serious game failed to surprise, amuse a little, irritate, awake the immense possibility that was offered with such simplicity, in those hours.

Of the speech that didn't happen, of the manner in which it would have received the being of the other without being harnessed by the self, now only the idea remains, in sum. This ungraspable light, which seems nearly a physical thing: nothing but an idea, no promise, none at all.

An idea? But I recognize, at least as much as I am conscious of doing so, having encountered its sense elsewhere and even everywhere; it is what any poetic undertaking forces us to comprehend. To catch a glimpse of a mode of being in the world where everything has an immediate and intimate relationship, of shared freedom, a relationship of presence to presence in sum, this is the first intuition, the wish, the beginning of poetry. But language comes along to commandeer the means of the exchange between men and women who attempt to speak to each other, to impose on them its own way of thinking, which is made by borrowing from each of them and from everything mere aspects, congealed appearance: and the dream immediately proliferates in the word, dream of self and dream of the other, and the glimpsed poetry reveals itself to be the inaccessible. It is itself and already poetry, this piece of mirror that a fatal hand, rising from the depths of language to settle over ours, incites us to abandon on the parapet of terraces.

Poetry is itself an idea. Of all its elans, all its calls, all these convictions mingled with illusions, all these pieces of writing whose purpose is an act of speech, but which soliloquy gets the best of, one must truly think that nothing remains in our lives save instants with no tomorrows, though with hope, nonetheless, which can brighten the colours of many a day. No transfiguration pierces the mirror. Of the shards found in the grass, splashed with rain, we don't with our fingers fashion the sparkling germ of the plant that the spirit, limited though it is, nonetheless gives us the desire to.

VII

But, this idea, what about discussing it? What if we focused on this constantly longed for impossibility, gave it back its gravity, which is to remember when words put it in danger of oblivion?

Everyone brings his or her portion of presentiments and forgotten things to a discussion about being's potential. From beneath the mirror shard of one day of adult life, on a terrace, on the edge of a ravine, conjure up again what a child perhaps imagined, but without yet being able to understand it. We are in a little garden in front of the lean-to where portraits and mirrors lie under the hoses, behind the watering cans. In the middle of this garden, there is a pump, an iron body and an arm that creaks when one pumps it, and in front of it a cube of stone older than the house and its street and everything one knows of the world. The water flows into a hollow scooped out in the stone, one can store it there; in summer, when it is already almost dark, you are sent to fetch the bottles left there to keep them cool, and this is a place that—can I say this in a single word?—exists, in the surrounding unreality. It is good to go down the ten or twelve steps at the kitchen door towards it, beyond it a bed of lettuce and leeks, earth above all, black earth drenched at each watering.

And it's even better to return here, after dinner, now that night has fallen. Looking back, what does one see? The back of the house, the facade that gives on to the yard, the ground floor, quite high all the same, over cellars and one floor above it, and above that, in the roof, two dormer windows. In this dormer lodged an elderly woman who had been a servant in some house in another city, and whom one called Mademoiselle Esther. One saw her only rarely, but she really existed, one ran into her at the well and sometimes she invited me to come and look at the bric-a-brac on her shelves. She even gave me some, what one calls biscuit ware.

Yes, this is the facade one sees, when one is by the pump and turns round. It is therefore night, the two or three windows over the basement are lit. What is going on behind them? Only the usual worries, along with the illness of one of the inhabitants now. Half-heard conversations, long silences but also unexpected laughter at times. Whatever one left behind when one came out here to the pump.

Why bring up this memory? Because in front of the pump, the earth, constantly trampled on, is almost bare of grass, like a floor of hard-packed earth, and it's black, but old nails and bits of charcoal poke up here and there. I scratch the earth with my finger, I extract a nail, I throw it away. And this bit of glass? Am I going to speak of a piece of broken mirror already, in which I might have trapped a moonbeam, and that I would have wanted bigger, so as to aim it over there, up there, make it penetrate the house, save the world? No, it's only a bit of broken windowpane, two sides of plain glass, with some bumps in it, nothing to go looking for pictures in, and even less to capture reflections in.

A year or two later, in the courtyard of my new middle school, I found a piece of board some five by seven centimetres large, a few millimetres thick, scrap wood left over from some carpentry work. I took this piece of wood, I took it seriously, I kept it for years. What am I going to say about it, whose two sides equally rejected whatever can be born of captive light, mirages, dreams, hopes—although not the ultimate, the irreducible? Nothing, save that I see in it, still today, the umbilicus, the centre to which everything goes back in the space granted me by words.

TRANSLATOR'S NOTES

I am grateful to Yves Bonnefoy for pointing out to me and discussing some of the echoes and allusions in his poems. In these notes I quote from *L'Inachevable*, a collection of interviews with the poet, many of which address questions of artistic creation, and from the texts in *Dans un débris de miroir*. I have also tried to give a glimpse of some earlier French poems to which Bonnefoy alludes. Unless otherwise mentioned, the translations are mine.

Strike Further

The sonnets in this section and in 'Be Love and Psyche' were first published in 2009 by Éditions Galilée with the title *Raturer outre*, a title I have found difficult to translate satisfactorily, for reasons of both sound and meaning: *raturer*—to cross out; *outre*—beyond, in addition to, as well as. In the original volume these sonnets were introduced by the following note (reproduced in *L'heure présente*, p. 119):

> Had I not adopted this prosodic approach, fourteen lines distributed over two quatrains and two tercets, these poems would not exist, which would not perhaps be a great loss, but I would not have known what someone inside me had to tell me.
>
> Words, words as such, granted their own sonic reality by the primacy of form, have established between themselves relationships I was far from imagining. The need, in this narrow space, to avoid the repetition—save deliberate—of the least vocable, effaced some thoughts and images, under which others appeared. The constraint has been a tendril, piercing levels of defense, giving access to memories that remained closed if not repressed.
>
> This is what I call 'raturer outre'. Form which puts itself rhetorically, and thus passively, to work in the service of what one thinks one knows and wishes to say, also proposes, poetically, to deconstruct these ideas, discovering, under them, other strata. A 'trobar', on language's strings.

I Give You these Lines . . .

See Charles Baudelaire, *The Flowers of Evil* (1857), poem 39: 'I give you these lines so that if my name . . .'

Stéphane Mallarmé (1877): 'Over the forgotten woods when sombre winter passes . . .; especially lines 9–12: Who wishes to receive visits must not / With too many flowers encumber the stone.'

Mallarmé, 'Crisis of Verse' (1896): 'I say a flower! And, from the oblivion to which the voice relegates every contour, inasmuch as it is something other than the known calyxes, arises, musically, the idea itself, suave, of that which is absent from every bouquet.'

The Missing Name

Proust's housekeeper: Céleste Albaret (1892–1984) was Marcel Proust's housekeeper for the last years of his life, and the author of *Monsieur Proust* (Paris: Éditions Robert Laffont, 1973).

The Garden

Pomona: Goddess of fruitfulness in Roman mythology (the French word for apple is *pomme* and the Latin *pomun* means the fruit of the orchard). In his recollection of Adrienne Monnier, the owner of the Paris bookstore, La Maison des Amis des Livres, on rue de l'Odéon, who welcomed so many writers to her shop, Bonnefoy calls her 'the Pomona of books, which were during these sad years [1944 . . .] the unbelievable fruits, the fruit saved, from times for me unknown'. ('Adrienne Monnier' in *Dans un débris de miroir*, pp. 97–100; here, p. 97)

The Red Scarf

a porch: In French, *une porche*, evokes an entryway, to a church, for example. For other implications of porch for Bonnefoy, see 'In a Piece of Broken Mirror' and its discussion of Mallarmé's prose poem, 'Winter Shiver' (1864–67).

The Revolution the Night

When I wondered how to translate the poem's title, pointing out that the juxtaposition of the two elements in the title could be translated in different ways—by simple juxtaposition, but also as 'The Revolution, the Night', and '(The) Revolution by/at Night', Bonnefoy, in a conversation in November 2011, said he would like to keep the juxtaposition of the two nouns, giving each equal weight and keeping the relationship between them ambiguous.

In his 2007 interview with Daniel Bergez, reprinted in *L'Inachevable* as 'Sur la création artistique' (On Artistic Creation; pp. 37–66), Bonnefoy discusses his 1987 poem 'Psyché devant le château d'Amour' (Psyche before Love's Castle). The poem, he says, 'clearly refers to Claude Lorrain's famous canvas'—*The Enchanted Castle* (1664)—but, he adds, 'in fact, it is only too clear that in this poem I am speaking of myself above all, dipping very far and very deep into my childhood memories.' (p. 64)

Pietà or Revolution by Night (1923) is a painting by Max Ernst, which depicts a bowler-hatted figure, generally considered to represent Ernst's father, holding another figure, probably his son, on his knees. The painting is thought to bear witness to Ernst's troubled relationship with his father.

La révolution la nuit was also a journal created in Paris in 1946 by Bonnefoy, then close to the surrealists, in which he published a fragment of his long poem *Le Coeur-espace* (Heart-Space; Tours: Éditions Farrago, 2001).

'*Father, don't you see I'm burning?*': A quotation from Sigmund Freud's dream study of 'The Burning Child'.

Hallway after hallway in his destiny: 'his' rather than 'its', as Bonnefoy clarified over email in October 2012.

Down at the end the avenue was red: Bonnefoy comments in 'Les ateliers de Tours' (Workshops in Tours; pp. 91–6), another memoir in *Dans un débris de miroir*, that his father 'laboured the whole of his too brief adult life in Tours' forges' (p. 94). Looking at a black-and-white photograph of the old railway hangars, Bonnefoy imagines the sun rising: 'this long red brushstroke where hope might have taken hold' (p. 92).

we didn't speak: In French, 'nous ne parlions pas'. When I discussed with Bonnefoy in November 2011 the translation of this phrase, which in French can mean both 'we didn't speak' or, with a harsher psychological emphasis, 'we weren't speaking', he said he wished to keep both meanings.

The Idea of a Book

In 'Les ateliers de Tours' again, Bonnefoy describes his father's work building locomotives and adds:

> We lived in one of the nearby streets, full of the sounds of trains and tracks, and my father, although he was rather taciturn, spoke to me sometimes of 'the shop'. [. . .] He liked to show me a book in which there were models of those locomotives, so varied in form, dimension, even their names . . . (p. 95)

The Bed, the Stones

the stone: In Provence, safre is the name of a soft sandstone. Helvetian safre dates from at least fourteen million years ago. Though difficult to locate in a dictionary, this word is used, even in English, in discussions of the terroir of certain Rhone wines. In a 1992 interview with Jean Roudaut, reprinted in *L'Inachevable* as 'Entretien avec Jean Roudaut' (Interview with Jean Roudaut; pp. 208–23), Bonnefoy says:

> I use the word 'safre' to designate a certain kind of sandstone, scattered about in large shapeless lumps—as they say, but shapelessness is a positive characteristic, an origin—that one encounters in a region dear to me and where it is called thus, which has led me to live it and love it under this name. Could I call it otherwise given that I am writing close to the bone, of course, of myself? (p. 214)

See also 'The Present Hour'.

Love and Psyche Again

This revisits 'Be Love and Psyche' and also 'Psyché devant le château d'Amour'. In 'Sur la création artistique', Bonnefoy says that 'Psyché devant le château d'Amour' asks the painter to explain 'what is at stake in the gaze that attempts to substitute the visible for the invisible. Isn't Psyche also like a child in the night?' (p. 65)

He Dismounts

Based on Gustav Mahler's *Das Lied von der Erde* ('Song of the Earth'; 1908–09), as interpreted by Kathleen Ferrier and Bruno Walter in 1925, one character in this poem has been feminized, Bonnefoy said in November 2011, to match Mahler's contralto singer.

Beauty

See Baudelaire, *The Flowers of Evil*, poem 17, in which Beauty speaks: 'I am beautiful, O mortals! like a dream of stone, / And my breast, where each in turn has been bruised, / Is made to inspire the poet with a love / As eternal and as mute as matter.'

Our Hands in the Water

That will 'change the sky', until evening: See Rimbaud's poem 'Tear' (1872): 'Far from birds, herds, the village girls, / I drank, squatting down in some heather / Surrounded by slender trunks of hazel, / In an afternoon fog lukewarm and green;' especially line 10: 'Then the storm changed the sky, until evening.'

He Reaches the High Seas

Written in memory of Jorge Luis Borges, this poem contains references to his tales, especially, 'The Form of the Sword' (1942) and 'The Garden of Forking Paths' (1944).

A Page from Robert Antelme

Robert Antelme: A member of the French Resistance, Antelme was arrested in 1944 and was deported to Buchenwald, and then to Gandersheim. His book *The Human Race* (1947) describes his experiences in the camps, including a poetry recital organized in Gandersheim by some of the prisoners.

I prefer thatch, he would say, to marble: A line from Joachim du Bellay, *The Regrets* (1558), poem 31:'Happy he who like Ulysses has made a fine voyage, / Or he who won the golden fleece / And returned, full of reason and usage, / To live with his family, the rest of his days!' It was recited by memory by one of the prisoners, as recounted in Antelme's book.

The Present Hour

The variations between lines and stanzas of the poem addressed to a *tu* and other lines addressed to a *vous*, which may suggest singularity versus plurality or intimacy versus formality, could not be captured in English. These forms of address, with regard to the identity of addressee (self, other?), are also at times ambiguous or polysemous in the French text.

My friend: In French, *mon amie*, the feminine form. Bonnefoy said in 2012 that it refers to the person with whom one shares one's life.

J. G. F.: Baudelaire's *Artificial Paradise* (1860) is dedicated to J. G. F., whom he addresses as 'Ma chère amie'. See also Bonnefoy's 'Le tombeau de Charles Baudelaire' (Charles Baudelaire's Tomb), in *La longue chaîne de l'ancre* (The Anchor's Long Chain; Paris: Mercure de France, 2008), especially the last two stanzas: 'Mysteriously you pointed to her / Because compassion is itself / The mystery that makes these three letters, // J, G, F, loom large in the light / On which your boat glides. To be for you / Harbour at last: its porticos, its palms.'

In our words: In French, 'Dans la parole'; *parole*, meaning 'word' and 'speech' has no exact equivalent in English. Bonnefoy suggested 'in our words' as the closest to his own sense of this line.

brain of gold: A reference to Alphonse Daudet's story 'La Légende de l'homme à la cervelle d'or' ('The Legend of the Man with the Golden Brain', 1868). Bonnefoy said in 2012 that he was filled with dread by this story when he read it as a child. The gift in Daudet's story was shoes; here it has been changed to a bouquet. The golden brain stands for *la pensée conceptuelle* (conceptual thinking).

chevêche: Owlet. Recall the owlet that flits through Wordsworth's 'The Idiot Boy'. Joseph Frank, in his 2003 tribute, 'Yves Bonnefoy: Notes of an Admirer', reprinted in Frank's *Responses to Modernity: Essays in the Politics of Culture* (New York: Fordham University Press, 2012, pp. 61–77), has remarked upon the ground Bonnefoy shares with Wordsworth: how in both, a single object may suddenly become 'charged with revelation' (p. 73). They also share an interest in childhood scenes as a wellspring of poetry. 'Un souvenir d'enfance de Wordsworth' (One of Wordsworth's Childhood Memories) is the title of a sonnet in *La longue chaîne de l'ancre*.

ciel: Sky, also heaven.

espérance: Hope

the broom / Flowering in the desert: See Giacomo Leopardi, *Canti*, 34: 'Broom, or the Flower of the Desert' (1845), a poem which is dominated by *Sterminator Vesevo* (exterminating Vesuvius).

In a Piece of Broken Mirror

a basement window: In French, *un soupirail*, a word which contains the verb *soupir*, 'to sigh'.

'*And your Venetian mirror . . .*': From Mallarmé's 'Winter Shiver'.